Rolls-Royce Silver Ghost (U.K., 1910)

Duesenberg Model J (U.S.A., 1934)

Cord Model 812 Custom Beverly sedan (U.S.A., 1937)

Morris M

many, c. 1965)—first built in 1936

Citroën DS21 Pallas sedan (France, 1967)

Bonneville Custom convertible (U.S.A., 1958)

THIS CAR

Paul Collicutt

Farrar Straus Giroux • New York

This book is for Penny and a car named Beryl

Distributed in Canada by Douglas & McIntyre Ltd.
Color separations by Hong Kong Scanner Arts
Printed and bound in the United States of America by Phoenix Color Corporation
Typography by Jennifer Crilly
First edition, 2002
1 3 5 7 9 10 8 6 4 2

Library of Congress Cataloging-in-Publication Data
Collicutt, Paul.
This car / Paul Collicutt.— 1st ed.
p. cm.
Summary: Simply describes a variety of cars, short and long, old and new, slow and fast.
ISBN 0-374-39965-4
1. Automobiles—Juvenile literature. [1. Automobiles.] I. Title.

TL147.C56 2002
629.222—dc21

2001054484

This car loops-the-loop.

This car is short.

This car is long.

This car is old.

This car is new.

This car is slow.

This car is fast.

This car has a closed top.

This car has an open top.

This car pulls a trailer.

This car pushes snow.

This car is solar-powered.

This car is gas-powered.

This car is down in a pit.

This car is up on a lift.

This car has no lights.

This car has many lights.

This car drives over water.

This car drives through water.

This car is lifted onto a boat.

This car is dropped from a plane.

This car is revving up . . .

ready to race!

Marmon Wasp (U.S.A., 1911)—
the world's first single-seater race car,
which won the first Indianapolis 500

Messerschmidt Tg500 Tiger
(Germany, 1957)—a "bubble car"

Streamlined 2.9-liter Alfa Romeo (Italy, 1938)—
raced in the Le Mans 24-hour race

Leyat saloon car (France, 1921)—
propeller-driven

Kurtis-Offenhauser (U.S.A., 1950)—
Indianapolis 500 race car

Mercedes W125 (Germany, 1937)

Airomobile (U.S.A., 1937)—ahead of its time with
an inexpensive air-cooled engine, front-wheel drive,
and only three wheels

Chevrolet Corvette (U.S.A., 1958)